PLAN OF THE CITADEL OF MYCENAE

**A** Grave Circle **Γ** Palace **Δ** Underground cistern **E** East wing of Palace

## Mycenae's Last Century of Greatness

In the summer of 1967 Professor George E. Mylonas made a thorough investigation of the so-called 'House of Columns' in the Citadel of Mycenae, originally revealed by Chrestos Tsountas and briefly described by Alan J. B. Wace in his *Mycenae, an Archaeological History and Guide*. Contrary to the generally accepted view, Professor Mylonas' investigation proves that the building was not a house but the centre unit of the east wing of the Palace, that it was constructed in the second half of the thirteenth century BC and that it was destroyed at the very end of that century. The construction of this unit is shown to have been a major undertaking which, added to the known works completed in the same period, demonstrates that at Mycenae prosperity and peace continued to exist to the end of the thirteenth century, and that this was the 'last century of greatness' for the city. The establishment of this unit's character made possible for the first time a reasonably accurate assessment of the area covered by the Palace and which now becomes the largest known royal establishment of the Mycenaean period in mainland Greece.

This illustrated study details the work and discusses the evidence presented by Professor Mylonas in the 1968 Myer Foundation Lecture, delivered in the University of Sydney under the auspices of the Australian Humanities Research Council.

Before his recent retirement Professor Mylonas was Chairman of the Department of the History of Art and Archaeology and Rosa May Distinguished University Professor in the Humanities of Washington University, St Louis, Missouri. He is the Director of Excavations at Mycenae.

Rock crystal cup, *c.* 1600 B C (Grave Circle B, Mycenae)

GEORGE E. MYLONAS

---

# *Mycenae's Last Century of Greatness*

SYDNEY UNIVERSITY PRESS
*for* AUSTRALIAN HUMANITIES RESEARCH COUNCIL
OCCASIONAL PAPER NUMBER 13

SYDNEY UNIVERSITY PRESS

*Press Building, University of Sydney*

NEW ZEALAND  Price Milburn and Company Limited
GREAT BRITAIN  Methuen and Company Limited, London
and their agents overseas

*First published* 1968
Copyright 1968 by George E. Mylonas
National Library of Australia registry number AUS 68-3202
Library of Congress Catalog Card Number 68-27810
SBN 424 05820 3
Printed in Australia at The Griffin Press, Adelaide
and registered in Australia for transmission by post as a book

# Illustrations

# *Preface*

Interest in Mycenae and in the Mycenaean Age has increased considerably in the last twenty years. Scarcely a year passes without the appearance of a book or articles, both learned and popular, dealing with the Cyclopean City. At the same time the epoch-making achievement of the late Michael Ventris in deciphering the Linear B Script increased the interest and widened the horizon of Mycenaean studies. Finally, the excavations being carried out with impressive results in various parts of Greece—at Mycenae, Tiryns, Pylos, Peristeria, Thebes, Thera, etc.—have added to the enthusiasm for these studies that originally was generated by Schliemann's lucky discovery in 1876.

As a result, the picture of the Mycenaean Age and of the Heroic Period of Greece is progressively being rounded off and our knowledge constantly enriched. To maintain that the picture is complete is not true neither will it be possible. There remain still many blank areas to be filled and many questions to be answered. None of these is more important or pressing than the questions raised by the revealed remains of the Palace of Mycenae. In 1886 that Palace was revealed by my late Professor Chrestos Tsountas of the University of Athens and its plan was drawn by the late Professor Wilhelm Dörpfeld. It was later cleared and studied by the late Professor Alan Wace of Cambridge University and a plan by L. Holland along with a full description was published by Wace. Its examination was resumed by Dr Spyros Iakovides, Professor T. Leslie Shear, Jr. and myself in the last ten years. In 1958-9, we revealed the main north stairway and the end of the road leading to it and to the Palace from the Lion Gate. In 1959 we examined and defined the northwest main entrance-propylon of the Palace and in 1960-3 we cleared once more the summit and determined the traces left on the rock by the Mycenaean construction. By 1964 it was believed that the extent of the Palace had been investigated. However, as the Palace stood then it seemed rather inadequate for the use of the most powerful king of the Late Mycenaean Age, of the ἄναξ ἀνδρῶν of Homeric poetry. The storage magazines, so characteristic of the 'Palace of Nestor' revealed by Professor Carl W. Blegen, were lacking and the compartments delineated by excavation seemed totally inadequate for the large household of a mighty ruler. It seemed to us that the 'Palace of Agamemnon' had not been revealed completely.

7

The work undertaken in the summers of 1965, 1966 and 1967 proved that the belief was justified. That work helps clear up a number of points connected with the Palace. It gives to it its exact and proper proportions; it sheds some light on the use of its many parts; it provides evidence dealing with the dates of its latest destructions; it gives us an insight into the artistic activity of the Palace household. Furthermore, it contributes to the solution of some problems connected with the life of the site in the thirteenth and twelfth centuries B C.

It is hoped that additional evidence will be obtained from the excavation, in the summer of 1968, of the section of the northeast slope of the hill that remains unexcavated. But it is already clear from the work completed, that in extent the Palace of Mycenae is the largest palace of the Mycenaean world, and that in spite of the lack of information regarding its earlier excavation, it is still yielding valuable information that increases considerably our knowledge of the Mycenaean Age.

I take this opportunity to express my deep appreciation and indebtedness to the Australian Humanities Research Council; its Chairman Professor R. M. Crawford and Secretary Dr K. V. Sinclair, and to the Myer Foundation for the opportunity extended to me to visit Australia and bring the story of Mycenae and of Eleusis to its people. My thanks are also due to the Sydney Association for Classical Archaeology and especially its Chairman Mr Arthur T. George. I am also grateful to the Administration of the University of Sydney and especially to its former Vice-Chancellor Sir Stephen Roberts and its present Vice-Chancellor Professor B. R. Williams for the chance to lecture to the students and discuss problems connected with the life of Greece in the dawn of history. To the vice-chancellors and members of the Classics departments of the Australian and New Zealand universities which my wife and I visited I wish to extend our heartfelt thanks. I am especially grateful to Professor Alexander Cambitoglou of Sydney University for his constant and unremitting efforts to ensure the success of my lecture tour. The friendship shown to us by the Australian people will remain to the end of our lives the high point of our experiences in their wonderful land. To the Sydney University Press Board, its Manager Mr Hugh Price, its Editor Mr Malcolm Titt, and its Design Editor Mr David New I wish to extend my thanks for the careful publication of my Myer Foundation Lecture.

Washington University                                        *George E. Mylonas*
St. Louis, Missouri

# Mycenae's Last Century of Greatness

M YCENAE, unlike Troy, was never completely buried and the location of its site did not become the subject of learned argumentation. (*See* endpapers for plan of the Citadel of Mycenae.) Its acropolis was always known and its guardian lions never left their post of vigilance (*Fig.* 1). We find Mycenae mentioned in the writings of the 'early travellers' to Greece in the closing years of the eighteenth century and the beginning of the nineteenth century of our era.[1] In 1840 after the liberation of Greece from the Ottoman Turks, the Greek Archaeological Society of Athens cleared the outer court of its acropolis and opened up its Lion Gate. Fate, however, had reserved the glory of bringing Mycenae back to light and life for Heinrich Schliemann who

[1] A. J. B. Wace, *BSA*, Vol.25 (1921-1923), p.283ff.

*Figure* 1    The Lion Gate before Schliemann's excavations. Drawing by W. Gell, *The Itinerary of Greece*, 1810, Pl. 11

in 1876 discovered and explored its royal cemetery, Grave Circle A as it is now known, filled with invaluable and almost mythical works of art.[2] Schliemann's discovery opened up a new horizon of Greece's life which is still being studied and explored. His work was followed by the more systematic researches of Chrestos Tsountas, Alan J. B. Wace, John Papadimitriou, and Nicholas Verdelis, to mention only those who are no longer with us, and is even now being continued under the auspices of the Greek Archaeological Society and of Washington University.

As a result of the work of international scholars the story of the life and achievement of Mycenae has been extended far beyond the chronological limits remembered by tradition, far beyond the years of Perseus, its legendary founder. Mycenae's two Grave Circles with their shaft graves dating from the end of the seventeenth to the end of the sixteenth centuries B C[3] disclosed not only its wealth but also a confidence in its strength which made possible the placing of so many valuable objects in graves beyond the confines of a citadel. They also proved that Crete was the cultural teacher and mentor of Mycenae.

Gradually the importance of Mycenae and of the other Mycenaean city states[4] increased and with the advent of the fifteenth century B C, the Mycenaeans began to take over the commercial activities of the Minoans in the eastern and the western areas of the Mediterranean. Finally, they established themselves in the Minoan trading posts and colonies and became even the masters of Knossos, the capital city of Minos, from which they ruled parts of Crete for generations.[5] It is not possible to determine the areas of the mainland from which these Mycenaeans started on their career of displacing the Minoans, but

[2] H. Schliemann, *Mycenae*, 1878, and G. Karo, *Die Schachtgraeber von Mykenai*, 1930-3.

[3] G. E. Mylonas, *Mycenae and the Mycenaean Age*, 1966, pp.99-107.

[4] Artefacts and works of art similar to those found at Mycenae have been discovered in many parts of the Greek world in the course of excavations carried out after the important discoveries of Schliemann and Tsountas. Scholars gave the name 'Mycenaean' to the culture and era represented by these artefacts, and the people who produced them are now known as Mycenaeans whether they lived at Mycenae or in the other city states of mainland Greece in the Late Bronze Age—from *c.* 1600 B C to *c.* 1120 B C.

[5] Sp. Marinatos, 'The Minoan and Mycenaean Civilization and its Influence on the Mediterranean and Europe', *Atti del VI Congresso Internazionale delle Scienze Preist.-Protostoriche*, Vol.I, (1961), p.161ff; S. Immerwahr, 'Mycenaean Trade and Colonization', *Archaeology*, Vol.13 (1960), p.4ff; M. Cavalier, 'Les cultures préhistoriques des îles Éoliennes et leur rapport avec le monde Égéen', *BCH*, Vol.84 (1960), p.319ff, and F. Stubbings, 'The Expansion of Mycenaean Civilization', rev. edn, *CAH*, Vols I and II, fasc. 26, p.18ff.

there can be little doubt that among them the people from Mycenae itself formed a most important element. At the same time the city of Mycenae began to develop independently in the artistic and cultural fields and embarked on the development and construction of an impregnable citadel and of impressive tholos tombs for its royal families.

The fourteenth century BC could be considered as the Golden Age of Mycenae but its growth and prosperity continued into the thirteenth century BC. Scholars specializing in the Mycenaean Age are in unanimous agreement regarding the gradual development of Mycenae and of the Mycenaean culture up to the middle of the thirteenth century BC. But there they part ways. Some maintain that after the middle of that century a change in the fortunes of Mycenae took place, that the Mycenaean world and Mycenae itself, its hub, were apprehensive of impending hostile assaults, that the expected incursions forced the people of Mycenae to add to the fortifications of their citadel, and that final disaster came at the end of the century.[6] I have pointed out that this concept is contrary to the facts as revealed by the latest excavations.[7] Prosperity and quiet continued to the end of the thirteenth century BC as indicated by the tablets of Pylos and the recent finds at Mycenae. Around the middle and in the second half of that century a number of great projects were carried out at Mycenae: the 'Treasury of Atreus', the 'Tomb of Klytemnestra'—beyond the walls of the citadel, the Lion Gate, and the 'Great Ramp' in the citadel itself. These could not have been produced by an apprehensive, threatened and economically declining community; their construction testifies to the pride and confident strength of a prosperous state. To the monuments and buildings enumerated by me[8] we may now add another important unit whose details were revealed in our campaign of the summer of 1967.

On the east slope of the acropolis of Mycenae the late Professor Chrestos Tsountas in 1892 revealed the remains of an imposing building which, in 1939, was cleared and studied again by the late Professor Alan J. B. Wace (*Fig. 3*). The latter gave us the only existing account and plan of the ruins of the building which, because of its many columns, he called the 'House of Columns'.[9] Tsountas, who excavated the area

[6]*Cf.* for example C. Nylander, 'The Fall of Troy', *Antiquity*, Vol.37 (1963), p.8ff; O. Broneer, *Hesperia*, Vol.8 (1939), p.426, and *Antiquity*, Vol.30 (1956), pp.16-17, and C. Blegen, *The Mycenaean Age*, pp.22-4. For a list and an account of destroyed Mycenaean sites *see* Per Ålin, *Das Ende der mykenischen Fundstätten auf dem griechischen Festland*, 1962 (*Studies in Mediterranean Archaeology*, Vol.I).

[7]Mylonas, *Mycenae and the Mycenaean Age*, p.223.       [8]ibid.

[9]A. J. B. Wace, *Mycenae, An Archaeological History and Guide*, 1949, pp.91-7 and figs 32-4.

of the building and cleared it of its fill, did not publish an account of his work and its results. Wace had little chance to dig unexcavated fill. As a result he did not attempt to date the construction of the 'House of Columns' and it was assumed that it was destroyed by fire at the end of the Mycenaean Age. In the summer of 1967 we undertook the final clearing and study of the building.

From Wace's publication it was known that the building was composed of two parts built on two different levels; one of these, the southeast section, built some 4.50 metres below the level of the second, was made up of storage magazines and corridors leading to them.[10] The walls of these magazines, lately strengthened and preserved, stand to a good height giving us a complete picture of the ground plan of the south section. On these magazines and on the level of the second section stood an upper storey, not preserved.

The second section was built on a terrace artificially constructed along the southeastern slope of the hill. On Wace's restored plan the second section occupies the areas A-P.[11] The terrace and its fill of stones were overlooked in the previous researches, and yet they have preserved evidence that might date the construction. To obtain that evidence, in the form of sherds thrown along and among the stones and earth which constitute the fill of the terrace, we undertook the removal of the stones of the fill from a trench some 3 metres broad running along the south retaining wall of the terrace (the wall at the bottom of our *Fig. 3*, to which doorway **R** on Wace's plan belongs). Our hopes were realized; a good number of sherds were found. The unexpected and surprising result of this work, however, was the disclosure of the depth of the fill. At the northwest end of our trench, approximately at the centre of the width of the court, we had to stop the extraction of stones at a depth of 1.75 metres because digging deeper would have endangered the stability of the retaining wall. At the southeast end of our trench we reached the amazing depth of 4.25 metres and still the fill continued downward (*Fig. 2*).

Simultaneously with our efforts in the trench we cleared the east side of the terrace on the abrupt slope of the southeastern area of the hill. Along that side runs the South Cyclopean Wall which was erroneously believed to have acted as the retaining wall of the terrace. But at the southeast section of the terrace we found a fragment of its actual

[10] ibid., p.94ff and fig. 34.
[11] ibid., pp.91-4 and figs 19, and 32-3.

> *Figure 2*    Fill at the southeast corner of the trench opened in the terrace supporting the central unit of the east wing

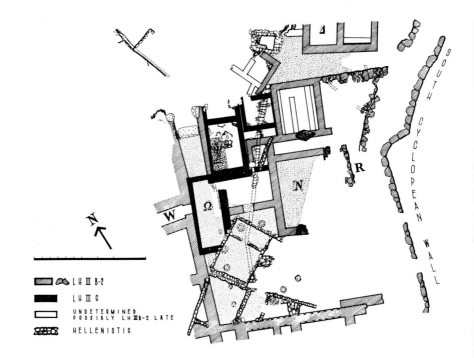

*Figure* 3    Plan of the central unit of the east wing.
**R** retaining wall. Drawing by Kenneth Schaar

retaining wall preserved to some 5.25 metres (*Figs* 3**R** and 4). In the area where this wall was revealed the fill would be at least 5 metres in depth. Furthermore the retaining wall helps determine the exact dimensions of the terrace which are 27 metres from north to south and 20.50 metres from east to west.[12] Thus the terrace is proved to be smaller in extent only to that constructed by the rulers of Mycenae on the southwest slope of the summit of the hill to act as a base for the megaron of the palace for its court and for the guest compartment.[13] And the type of its fill is proved to be identical to that of the summit. It is evident that the construction of the terrace required an immense amount of stone and represents an activity beyond the means of a mere citizen, rich though he might have been, and suggests the activity of a

[12] Actually the building and its terrace are oriented from northeast to southwest, but for the sake of clarity and simplicity we shall use the directions 'north' and 'south'. The exact determination of the extent of the terrace to the southeast makes Wace's restoration of the ground plan of the unit impossible and invalidates his statements regarding its similarity to the 'House of Odysseus'.

[13] G. E. Mylonas, *Ancient Mycenae*, p.41ff, and *Mycenae and the Mycenaean Age*, p.58ff.

R

*Figure* 4 Southeast side of terrace supporting the
central unit. **R** retaining wall

ruler. From the terrace alone one could conclude that the building
known as the 'House of Columns' was not a house, as the term is
generally understood.

Other aspects of its construction lead us to the same conclusion. The
stone fill of the terrace in its entire extent, some 550 square metres, was
covered by a layer, averaging 0.10 metres in thickness, of water-
resisting clay known to the villagers as *plesia*. That clay was brought to
the citadel from a distance of two kilometres. Over the *plesia* was placed
a thick layer of earth some 0.70 metres in thickness. That earth, known
to the villagers as *belitsa*, is very hard and was composed, in the course
of millenia, of deteriorated rock; it is to be found at a distance of one
and a half kilometres from the acropolis. Over the *belitsa* was laid the

*Figure* 5    Base and foundations of column No. 2 in the court

*Figure* 6   Entrance to the central unit of the east wing
of the Palace. View from north. **a** prothyron **b** threshold
**c** corridor **d** and **e** LH III C walls

Mycenaean lime cement that formed the pavements of the court and
of the apartments of the building. The work involved in the making of
the substructure of the pavements again indicates a royal activity.

   The same care and attention was given to the columns of the court.
Their bases, of rounded conglomerate stone, were set securely on a
carefully constructed stone foundation that was placed on top of the
*plesia* layer (*Fig.* 5). No private house of the Mycenaean era exhibits
either a similar care for column bases or a comparable number of
columns resting on them. The details in the plan of the building point
to the same conclusion. The unique *prothyron* of the building,[14] the wide

[14]Wace, *Mycenae* figs 33A, and our *Figs* 3 and 6.

main corridor (some 2.70 metres wide at its beginning) well paved with lime cement (*Fig.* 6), the two contiguous megara[15] which formed its apartments on the ground floor, and its colonnaded and well-paved court (*Fig.* 7), are not to be found in a house but belong to a section of the palace. Note especially the size of the court. The west half measures some 11 metres by 9.50 metres; the east half 9.50 metres by 9.50 metres; the maximum width is 19 metres and the maximum length is 11 metres. These dimensions compare favourably with those of the great court before the megaron of the palace section on the summit of the citadel which amount to 11 metres by 15 metres as restored, with those of the court of the palace of Tiryns that are 15.75 metres by 20.25 metres and those of the court before the megaron of the Palace of Nestor at Pylos that amount only to 12.90 metres by 7.30 metres.[16]

All these details lead to the same conclusion: the so-called 'House of Columns' is not the house of a noble or of a private individual but a part of the palace, the central part of the east wing of the palace which, as I have shown elsewhere, extended uninterruptedly from the megaron on the summit of the hill.[17] To this east wing belongs the structure first explored by Tsountas and revealed again in 1965, which with good reason, I hope, I called the 'Building of the Artisans and Artists' of the palace. The fortunate preservation and discovery in 1967 of a piece of plaster in its original position on the burnt west wall of the corridor leading to the court of the central part of the east wing (*Fig.* 8) resulted in the discovery of a doorway some 1.50 metres in width that led into the horizontal front corridor of the 'Building of the Artisans and Artists' (*Fig.* 3**W**). Thus the two buildings were connected and of the two our building is proved by its plan and construction to be the more important, hence the central unit of the wing. The door opening was not detected before because it was blocked by a single layer of stones belonging to a later wall built in front of it (*Fig.* 8**b**).

Again, the position of our unit in relation to two buildings to the north and northeast of it, buildings Gamma (*Γ*) and Delta (*Δ*) (*Fig.* 9), which we cleared in 1966 and 1967, and which are proved to have been made up of a great number of magazines for storage, indicates its

[15] ibid., fig. 33F, G, H and N.
[16] W. Dörpfeld, in Schliemann, *Tiryns*, p.203, and C. W. Blegen and M. Rawson, *The Palace of Nestor at Pylos in Western Messenia*, p.63.
[17] G. E. Mylonas, 'The East Wing of the Palace of Mycenae' in *Hesperia*, Vol.35 (1966), pp.419-26.

*Figure* 7   Column bases in the court of the LH III B-2 building. View from north. **e** LH III C walls

*Figure* 8    West wall of corridor leading to the court
of the central unit of the east wing. View from east.
**a** plaster on LH III B-2 wall **b** LH III C blocking wall
**c** entrance to corridor **W d** corridor **W**

central and important character. The general conclusion indicated by
all the evidence is that what we have previously called the 'House of
Columns' was the central unit of the east wing of the palace. The extent
of that palace can now be established for the first time. It covered not
only the summit of the hill, as was believed, an area that is only 50
metres by 70 metres in maximum extent, but its eastern slope as well.
Its extreme length from east to west amounted to some 170 metres, while
its width from north to south ranged from 50 metres to 80 metres. Thus,
it is proved to be the largest palace on the mainland of Greece,[18] a

18 The Palace of Nestor at Pylos measures 85 metres by 70 metres.

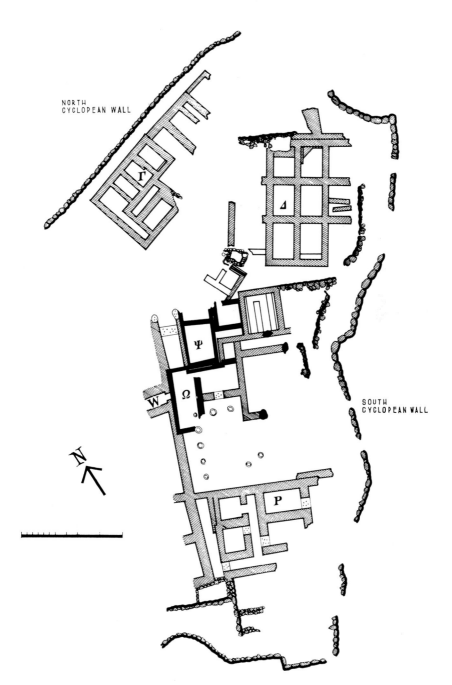

*Figure* 9    The central unit in relation to buildings
Gamma (*Γ*) and Delta (*Δ*). Drawing by Kenneth Schaar

21

*Figure* 10    Painted sherds from the stone fill of the
terrace supporting the central unit

*Figure* 11    South retaining wall of the terrace
with chases for wooden beams

fitting residence and symbol of the mightiest *wanax* of the Mycenaean
world.

As we have seen above, in the fill of the terrace were found a good
many sherds most of which were plain, but painted examples are among
them in sufficient number to prove the date of the construction of our
unit (*Fig.* 10). All the sherds found belong to the ceramic phase known
as Late Helladic III B (LH III B) and the latest among them belong
to the second half of the B phase, that is to the second half of the
thirteenth century BC. The latest examples date the fill and the
terrace, consequently the building on that terrace also must have been
constructed in the second half of the thirteenth century BC. It seems
that an older building existed where the terrace was constructed,
because the south retaining wall of the terrace, when it was revealed,
showed chases for the insertion of wooden beams used in the construction (*Fig.* 11). The top of the wall, as it survives, is level with the floor

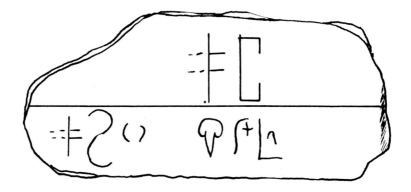

*Figure* 12    Inscribed tablet from the 'Pithos Basement'

of the court, consequently the beams were below that floor. Their presence can be explained only if we deduce that at the time of its construction an empty space existed along the face of that wall, otherwise the beams would have been exposed to the moisture that would accumulate naturally in an artificial fill. That empty space could only have been a room of a structure that was filled up when the terrace was constructed. The few sherds that came from the retaining wall, from around the chases, belong to the LH III B period indicating that the assumed building was earlier than the terrace.

This is further indicated by the existing 'Pithos Basement' on the other side of the retaining wall, cleared by Wace. The re-examination of that basement disclosed the existence of an earlier and of a later floor belonging to two different phases of the LH III B period. On the later floor, with a number of sherds and two painted terracotta animal figurines, we found the greater part of an inscribed tablet (*Fig.* 12) the face of which is divided by a horizontal line in two registers. On the lower register the inscription reads *pa-we-a ko-u-ra* (garments of light weight) placing the tablet in the Lc series.[19] The later floor, with the tablet and sherds, is contemporary with the terrace. The earlier floor belongs to an older structure to which must belong the assumed room below the terrace. At any rate the terrace and the building erected over it belong to the second half of the thirteenth century BC.

When we recall the amount of labour its construction involved, we can safely conclude that this building was a major undertaking that would presuppose prosperous economic conditions and internal security. Could people harassed by hostile invasions, or living in fear of such invasions, have undertaken such a major construction? If this is added to the other projects conceived and carried out in that same half-century it would demonstrate that the hypothesis of declining economic conditions and increasing fear of war in that time is untenable. The thirteenth century BC throughout its extent is proved by the archaeological evidence to have been a century of prosperity and greatness for Mycenae. Was this its last century of greatness?

The calcined walls prove that the so-called 'House of Columns' of the LH III B-2 period was destroyed by fire, but the date of its destruction remained uncertain. The unit must have been destroyed at the same time as the 'Building of the Artisans and Artists' adjacent to it. A few painted sherds found in the undug fill of that building in 1965 indicated a date at the very end of the LH III B period.[20] This was confirmed by a fortunate find in 1967. In the fill preserved under a Hellenistic wall whose stones collapsed in the course of the winter and spring, and on the burnt surface of the floor of the court, we found a

---

[19] Michael Ventris and John Chadwick, *Documents in Mycenaean Greek*, p.313ff.

[20] Mylonas, 'The East Wing of the Palace of Mycenae' in *Hesperia*, Vol.35 (1966), p.426 and pl. 96b. Perhaps we may note here that dating earlier and later destructions by sherds only is not a safe method of procedure. Sherds, along with hay and other grit, were inserted in the making of mud bricks used in the construction of walls. The dissolution of these bricks formed part of the fill which necessarily includes the sherds contained in them; consequently some of the sherds found in a fill would date the construction rather than the destruction of the building in whose bricks they were used. Floor deposits are the only safe and accurate evidence of a destruction and on them should be based our dates.

*Figure* 13   Nest of sherds on the floor of the court
of the 'Building of the Artisans and Artists'

nest of broken pottery consisting of the greater part of three false-necked
amphorae (*Fig.* 13). They are of the type called by Professor Carl W.
Blegen amphorae with pedestal base and characterize the very last
years of the LH III B period.[21] To the closing years of that period must
be attributed the destruction of the 'Building of the Artisans and
Artists' and of the central unit of the east wing of the palace.

On the north slope of the citadel just below these two structures an
undisturbed fill of considerable size was located at the end of last
summer's work (1967). Part of this is made up of broken pottery and
other objects that rolled down the slope after the destruction. We
cleared only a small strip of this fill to determine its nature and it

[21] Blegen and Rawson, *The Palace of Nestor at Pylos in Western Messenia*, p.410 and
figs 391 and 392.

26

yielded a mass of broken pottery that is now being put together (*Fig.* 14). Our preliminary study indicates that the destruction which the pottery illustrates occurred at the very end of the LH III B period; thus it confirms the results obtained in the 'Building of the Artisans and Artists'. We may, therefore, with confidence accept as a fact that the east wing of the palace was destroyed by fire in the last years of the LH III B period.

This destruction is not limited to the east wing only. Other buildings within and without the acropolis were destroyed by fire in the same years. Elsewhere, too, in the Argolid, in Tiryns for example, destructions seem to have occurred in those years.[22] And the question is asked what brought about these destructions. This is a problem to which various solutions have been suggested, none of which has been unanimously accepted so far. A good many scholars believe that the destruction was wrought by outsiders, by the 'Sea Peoples' of the Egyptian documents attacking from the sea; others believe that it was the result of the so-called 'Illyrian Migration' of people coming by land from southwest Europe seeking to occupy new territories, while still others attributed it to the Dorians of the tradition. I have pointed out in my book[23] that it would have been impossible for any invaders to have reached Mycenae undetected and to have destroyed first its citadel and then that of Tiryns, or vice versa. Perhaps the mysterious 'Sea People' could have destroyed Tiryns, but to maintain that afterwards they marched inland and destroyed Mycenae is untenable; the mere force required for this military feat is prohibitive for sea raiders. Again to maintain that vast crowds of migrants, carrying their belongings along with their wives and children, could have reached undetected the territory of Mycenae surprising its defenders is beyond belief. It is well known that Mycenae kept a number of roads to the north looked after by guard towers and houses whose sentinels would have apprised the people at home of any impending incursion, and the look-out post on top of Mount Elias, with its wide view of the entire territory, was still maintained at the time. The same reasoning applies to the Dorians also, but now against this Dorian destruction we have not only a new argument but new evidence.

In 1957 Professor Oscar Broneer discovered at Isthmia a fragment of a cyclopean wall which, according to the discoverer, originally stretched across the Isthmus.[24] It is stated that the fear of approaching

[22] P. Ålin, *Das Ende der mykenischen Fundstätten auf dem griechischen Festland*, 1962, p.10ff.
[23] Mylonas, *Mycenae and the Mycenaean Age*, 1966, pp.224-9.
[24] Broneer, *Antiquity*, Vol.32 (1958), pp.80-9, fig. 2, and *Hesperia*, Vol.28 (1959), p.298ff.

danger and impending incursions of the Dorians motivated its construction. On the basis of the pottery found in the wall Professor Broneer, in a recent article, has specifically stated that the wall was built in the transitional period from LH III B to LH III C;[25] the type of construction illustrated by the wall confirms this date. But as we have seen, the destruction at Mycenae occurred at the very end of the LH III B period. How then can it be attributed to the Dorians if a wall was being built in the transitional period from LH III B to III C, to guard Corinthia and the Argolid from incursions of the Dorians, which were still expected, which were still to come? If Mycenae and Tiryns were destroyed by the Dorians at the very end of LH III B then we have to accept as a fact that these Dorians had penetrated a territory farther south from the Isthmus and had taken control of the land; for we could not assume that having destroyed those strongholds they withdrew to the north of the Isthmus. If the Dorians had penetrated as far south as Mycenae and Tiryns and had taken control of the land then the building of a wall to protect this land from such a penetration in the course of the transitional period from LH III B to III C would have been superfluous. It seems to us that the wall found at Isthmia excludes the Dorians as the destroyers of Mycenae at the very end of the LH III B period. We believe that the only possible explanation of the destruction is that suggested by the legends of Mycenae;[26] the struggle for power among members of the royal family and their supporters, the successive elimination by murder of members of that

[25] *Hesperia*, Vol.35 (1966), p.354.
[26] Mylonas, *Mycenae and the Mycenaean Age*, 1966, p.226, in spite of Mr M. I. Finley's rejection of myths other than his own. Though an historian, he cannot realize how internal struggle can result in catastrophes as great as those characterizing the years around 1200 BC. I would like to point out to him a modern instance, thoroughly documented, from the life of Greece itself. In the struggle that followed the attempt of the communists to take over Greece at the end of World War II more men were killed than in the war itself (1,025 officers and 14,535 men as against 678 officers and 13,435). 4,123 non-combatant citizens and 165 priests were killed, 40,000 as against 11,750 were wounded and 30,000 children were abducted to communist countries. The damage caused in burned villages and houses, in the destruction of bridges, railways etc., exceeds three and a half billions of drachmae. Of course, some, including unfortunately historians, prefer to ignore these facts. Nevertheless they do exist and are available, in Greece as well as elsewhere (see what happens in China) to prove the destructive nature of internal struggle for the assumption or the keeping of power.

*Figure* 14    Sherds at the bottom of the north slope trench opened in 1967 below the east wing

family which weakened the prestige of the office of the king and plunged the state into civil war and temporary anarchy.

What happened at Mycenae in the twelfth century B C confirms this conclusion. Both archaeological and anthropological evidence prove that the same people continued to live at Mycenae after the great destruction of about 1200 B C. They produced the same type of pottery, although perhaps somewhat poorer in quality; they built their homes in the same way as before, although on a smaller scale; they buried their dead in chamber tombs, following the same rites as before, although the kterismata now became fewer, but included clay figurines which characterize the Late Mycenaean culture.[27] They no longer built tholos tombs, but perhaps this was due to the fact that what they had (the last tholos tomb was built towards the end of the thirteenth century) filled the need, and because people were poorer and could no longer afford tholos tombs for their kings. But their fortification walls were intact and they used the storage rooms within the North Cyclopean Wall and the corridors along that wall.[28] They seem to have built more structures within the acropolis. The evidence points to the fact that the people then were in poorer economic conditions, but continued to produce artefacts on the ancestral cultural lines and actually tried to recuperate from their misfortune and regain their old role of leadership. What seems to emerge from the latest excavations is that they built more structures and of better quality within the acropolis than we assumed before. Did they rebuild the palace on the summit, assuming that palace was totally destroyed around 1200 B C?

Unfortunately evidence was not recorded nor has it survived to tell us what happened to the palace on the summit. Wace maintained that it still existed in the twelfth century, that it was finally destroyed by fire only at the end of that century, at the end of the LH III C period.[29] However, the evidence he managed to find consists of sherds that remain unpublished and a deep, two-handled bowl which he attributes to the LH III C,[30] but which Lord William Taylour places at the end of the LH III B period. In our efforts to clear the summit completely

[27]Dr R. A. Higgins, of the British Museum, in his recent book on *Greek Terracottas* erroneously attributes to me, on p.13, the equation of the Mycenaean figurines with the ushebtis of Egypt, maintained by Axel Persson and Martin Nilsson. As a matter of fact, I tried to prove, successfully I hope, that these figurines could not be equated with the Egyptian ushebtis, that they represent divinities and divine nurses.

[28] *Praktika*, (1962), pp.62-4, pls 59-60.

[29] Wace, *BSA*, Vol.51 (1956), p.105, and 'Last Days of Mycenae' in *Aegean and the Near East*, p.126ff.

[30] *BSA*, Vol.51 (1956), p.105, fig. 2, and *Mycenaean Tablets*, III, p.46.

we found no other ceramic evidence. But if the east wing of the palace was destroyed by fire at the very end of the LH III B period there is the probability that the rest of the palace suffered the same fate at the same time. And the question can be raised whether or not the palace was rebuilt in the twelfth century BC, in LH III C times.

There is a slight pointer to strengthen the view that at least part of the palace on the uppermost terrace was rebuilt. There is a compartment on the summit of the hill known as the 'Pithos Room' because fragments of pithoi were found by Wace in their original position on the last floor of the room. Below that floor, however, we found in 1963 remains of an older floor covered with badly burnt gypsum slabs (*Fig.* 15). Similar gypsum slabs were employed for the floors of the megaron

*Figure* 15   Floors of the 'Pithos Room' on the summit of the Citadel. **a** later floor of lime cement **b** earlier floor of gypsum slabs

31

of the palace. They too exhibit strong signs of firing. It seems that the older floor of the 'Pithos Room' belongs to the years of construction in which were laid the floors of the megaron. The former was burnt and it was later replaced by another floor in which pithoi were set. Furthermore, the east wall of the 'Pithos Room' presents two periods of construction: to an older wall, that was badly burnt, was added a length of a later wall to strengthen its north end. The burnt wall belongs to the floor with the gypsum slabs, the additional strengthening wall goes with the later floor. The strengthening wall and the later floor were built after the destruction by fire of the room with the gypsum slab flooring. Furthermore, the later addition does not follow exactly the direction of the older wall but slants towards the west; it is, however, exactly oriented to the walls of the propylon of the northwest entrance. This may indicate that the northwest entrance was either rebuilt after the destruction of 1200 BC or survived that catastrophe. This is all the evidence we have from the summit and the inferences that can be deduced from it, of course, are not many, but point to the possibility that the part of the palace on the summit may have been rebuilt after the great disaster of 1200 BC.

The work carried out during the summer of 1967 has contributed more definite evidence regarding the east wing of the palace, and of the part occupied by its central building, the so-called 'House of Columns'. That building, as we have seen, was built in the second half of the LH III B period and was destroyed by fire in the last years of that period. Over its charred remains Tsountas disclosed (and Wace plotted and described) a number of walls which he distinguished into two groups. To the first group belong walls of a building constructed in Hellenistic times, in the third century BC. To the second were assigned all other walls and these were called post-Mycenaean;[31] thus Wace left their date uncertain but declared them to be non-Mycenaean. We cleared these walls once more (*Figs* 16 and 3) and found additional walls, proved to belong to definite buildings of one period, built over the burnt remains of the LH III B-2 central building; in some instances they were constructed on the burnt walls of the building which preceded them. Of course, nothing survived of their floors and of their contents, but the clearing of these walls and the unearthing for the first time of others yielded an amount of sherds sufficient to date them (*Fig.* 17). They belong to the last phase of the ceramic development of the Mycenaean Age, or the LH III C period that covers the twelfth century BC, and actually to the first part of that ceramic phase. It is

[31] Wace, *Mycenae*, fig. 32. In our *Fig.* 3 the LH III C walls are indicated by solid black colour.

*Figure* 16　Walls and column bases of the LH III B-2
and LH III C buildings. View from east. **a** threshold
of the LH III B-2 megaron **b** base of the portico of the
megaron **c** base of the LH III B-2 court
**d** walls of the LH III C building **e** wall of the
LH III C building **f** Hellenistic wall

interesting to note that among them are not to be found examples of
the so-called 'Granary' style, but all exhibit details common to the
pottery of the closing years of the LH III B phase plus the characteristic
colouring of the interior of the pots typical of the III C period. The
pottery then seems to prove that these walls and the buildings of which
they form a part not only belong to the twelfth century B C but also
that they were constructed in the early part of that century.

It is proved that then a small building, to be known as Psi (*Figs* 3
and 9, Ψ) was constructed along the east wall of the corridor of the

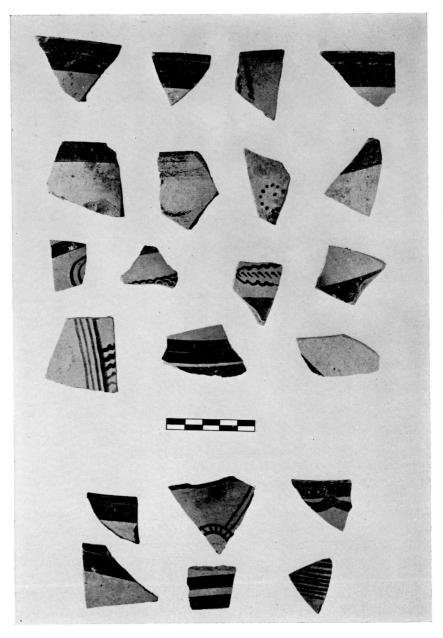

*Figure* 17    LH III C sherds from walls (upper
four rows) and base of column (lower two rows).
(Inner face of all sherds painted black)

*Figure* 18    Preserved walls and floor of LH III C
building Psi ( Ψ ). **h** hearth paved with sherds

LH III B-2 building, using that repaired wall for its west boundary
(*Fig.* 18). It seems to have consisted of a megaron-shaped apartment
with a domos some 5.60 metres by 3.75 metres fronted perhaps by a
portico that has not survived. It faced north and had a floor of earth,
*plesia* and lime—the pseudo-Mycenaean lime-concrete characteristic
of twelfth-century constructions. This building was dug before except
for a small section of its floor, some 4 metres in length and 1.70 metres
in width because a fragment of a Hellenistic wall stood over it. We
removed that wall and so we were able to clear the preserved floor.
Besides sherds (*Fig.* 19) a section of its fireplace paved with pottery
was found. When the latter was removed and cleaned it was found that
it originally belonged to a chimney-pipe that most probably stood
over the fireplace of the LH III B-2 megaron.

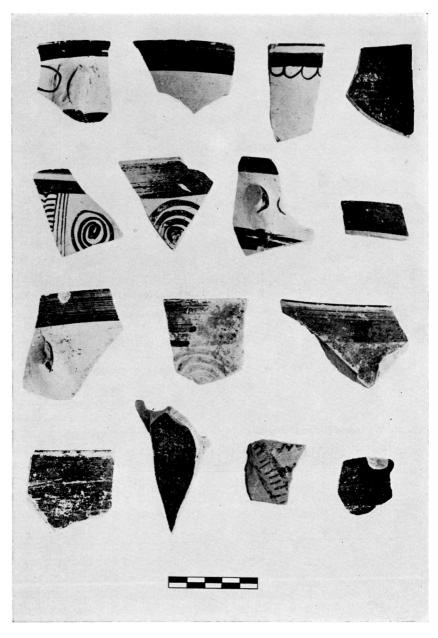

*Figure* 19    LH III C sherds from building Psi ( **Ψ** ).
(Inner face of all sherds painted black)

More ambitious was a second building, now called Omega, constructed shortly after Psi, over the corridor, the court and the megaron of the LH III B building (*Figs* 3 and 9, *Ω*). Its proportions, its capacity, and its character indicate that it was one of the important structures of the III C period; apparently a building erected to replace the destroyed central unit of the east wing of the palace. It comprises a large room, some 7 metres in length and 5.70 metres in width, along the west side of which existed a long and somewhat narrow thalamos, measuring 8.25 metres in length and 3.30 metres in width. Its entrance, not preserved, must have been on the south side, facing the open court.

*Figure* 20    Fragment of a threshold block re-used
as a column base in the LH III C building

37

On the east side of this main room, using the east wall of the LH III B-2 apartment, another was constructed some 8.20 metres in length and 6.10 metres in width, indicated in Wace's restored plan by the letter **N** (*Figs* 3, **N** and 9). It faced south and the court, and in its front were apparently two columns in antis; for the fragment of a conglomerate block that was assumed to have been part of the threshold of apartment **N** actually is the base of a column still sitting on the bedding prepared for it (*Fig*. 20). Among the wedging stones of its foundation, sherds were found belonging to the LH III C period (*Fig*. 17). Thus, it seems that in rebuilding the destroyed central unit the later builders followed in general the arrangement of the previous unit with the two contiguous megara, eliminating the entrance and corridor of the older structure, but using the lime floors of the older structure wherever they survived. And one wonders whether they did not attempt to do the same on the summit of the hill, to rebuild, that is, the main part of the palace, if that part was also destroyed at the very end of the thirteenth century B C. Unfortunately, due to the complete clearance of the summit in the early days of the excavations at Mycenae, the answer to this problem will remain unknown.

There can be no doubt, however, that early in the twelfth century B C, in LH III C times, the people of Mycenae tried to rebuild the central unit of the east wing of the palace following somewhat different lines but a similar ambitious palatial trend. This, the pottery found, and the use of the cyclopean walls, would seem to indicate that the people of Mycenae did try to recover the position of prestige and artistic importance they enjoyed in the thirteenth century B C, that they made a start towards attaining their objective, but that they were never able to reach it. They seem gradually to have declined until their citadel was destroyed totally and their political and cultural pre-eminence came to a final end. This gradual decline, I maintain, was due to the uncertain times brought about in Corinthia and the Argolid in the twelfth century B C by the raiding and infiltrating tactics of the Dorians. Those raiders, in spite of the wall at the Isthmus, kept the people pre-occupied with the defence of their property and homes and prevented them from recuperating fully and attaining their objective of regaining the high degree of prosperity and culture they enjoyed in the past. It seems that in Mycenae at the end of the thirteenth and in the course of the twelfth centuries B C we have exemplified the fact that internal struggle and division bring with them the seeds of destruction. Towards the end of the twelfth century B C the Dorians succeeded in capturing, perhaps by treachery, the citadels of Mycenae and of Tiryns. They managed to destroy those strongholds and thus were able to consolidate their occupation of the land and secure the safety and leadership of the new Dorian cities of Argos, Corinth, and Sparta.

The twelfth century B C was a period of decline, while the thirteenth is proved to have been the last century of greatness for Mycenae, the capital city of Agamemnon.